MW01231555

HOW FIRM A FOUNDATION

Cathy Butler

Woman's Missionary Union
Birmingham, Alabama

Woman's Missionary Union
P. O. Box 830010
Birmingham, AL 35283-0010

Dewey Decimal Classification: 266.023
Subject Headings: MISSIONS, FOREIGN
                  MISSIONS—AFRICA

Design by Janell E. Young
Cover design by Teresa Brooks
Photo credits: pp. 4, 7, 12, 35–42, 45, 46, 56, 61, International
    Mission Board (IMB); pp. 6, 10, 11, 26, 31, Faith Caddis;
    p. 8, Amy Giles

ISBN: 1-56309-543-2
W014117•0501•12.5M1

CONTENTS

How Firm a Foundation is course CG-0693 in the Christian
Growth Study Plan in the subject area Missions.

INTRODUCTION

"But you will receive power when the Holy Spirit comes on you; and you will be my witnesses in Jerusalem . . . and to the ends of the earth" (Acts 1:8 NIV).

To North American Christians, the Maasai [MAH-sigh] people might seem to live at the ends of the earth. Historically the Maasai are warriors and cattle herders, unburdened by the need to own land or put down roots. For generations they have roamed the grasslands of the Rift Valley in East Africa, making war on their enemies and raiding their enemies' cattle herds as well as tending their own flocks and herds.

But in the twenty-first century, the earth is a more crowded place than it was in New Testament days. The quarter of a million Maasai now feel the pressure of the rest of the world as it closes in on their grazing lands. Maasailand covers parts of

Kenya and Tanzania. Nairobi, Kenya's capital city, is expanding its city limits and taking in more territory. Game preserves and national parks are being carved out of the grasslands for the welfare of future generations of

Africans. Busloads of tourists now crisscross the valleys that the Maasai once shared only with their animals. Governments are urging the Maasai to settle in one place.

Added to these pressures is the strain of periodic droughts that force the Maasai farther and farther afield in search of grass and water for their herds. The most recent drought has been one of the worst ever, and the herds, the anchor of the Maasai way of life, have been devastated.

The Maasai want to retain their identity as a people. They are proud (some have called them arrogant) and historically have been resistant to outside forces, including the gospel. Some want to blot out the rest of the world, but others know that is not possible. They want the Maasai to still be Maasai, but they realize they are not at "the ends of the earth." They accept the need to prepare for new realities. Twenty years ago young Maasai who chose to go to school faced ridicule by their fellow tribe members. Now the wisdom of these men is apparent as many of them take their places as tribal leaders in the new world the Maasai face.

About 10 percent of Maasai in Kenya have become Christian. Building upon many years of work by veteran missionaries, today's missionaries work with an ever-strengthening Maasai church to spread the gospel. The Maasai themselves are planting churches and witnessing to their people. This working of God that occurs when a people group begins to rapidly plant its own churches is called a church planting movement (CPM).

A CPM is an exponential rather than incremental growth in indigenous churches. This means the churches multiply other churches rather than a missionary or national church planter adding one church at a time. To understand this phenomenon, imagine doubling a penny every day for a month. Initially it may not seem impressive—at the end of the first week you would still have only 64 cents. But by the end of a month you would have a fortune.

Many people groups throughout the world are experiencing CPMs. This International Mission Study focuses solely on the Maasai, mainly those residing in Kenya, and the missionaries who today work with them and bear witness to the power of God moving through the Maasai. Through learning about the Maasai you can be part of this work as you pray for them and for the missionaries, as you give to missions, and as you do missions yourself. The Maasai and peoples like them will no longer seem like just pictures out of *National Geographic,* set in some exotic place "at the ends of the earth." You will see them for what they really are, your brothers and sisters in Christ, following the New Testament model of expanding Christ's church.

1

WHO ARE THE MAASAI?

The Lord is my shepherd, I shall not want
(Psalm 23: 1).

I t is part of God's great providence that His Word contains so many references that the Maasai, a seminomadic tribe in East Africa, can understand. The Maasai are proud to be animal herders. They spend their lives in close contact with their cattle, goats, and sheep. The words of David, the shepherd poet, echo their own concern for the most basic needs—water, grass, protection from threat. As the Spirit of God moves throughout the Maasai people, more and more are also coming to understand the words of Christ: "I am the good shepherd."

The Maasai are probably one of the better known African tribal people, at least by name, and are often depicted in movies like *Out of Africa*. Often they are shown as fighting against the British who colonized their homelands. This is part of the picture, for the Maasai are a warrior culture. When Europeans encroached on their lands in the mid-nineteenth century, they resisted, but to no avail. Famine and smallpox ravaged them. Their cattle herds, the basis of their wealth, were weakened by a disease called rinderpest, another European import into Africa. In the early twentieth century the British were able to relocate the Maasai to southern Kenya and Tanzania. They remain there today in an area called Maasailand.

The Maasai are recognized by their tall, lean build and the red, blanket-type drape they wear. They also wear colorful bead necklaces, earrings, and bracelets. These beads help signify which subtribe, or clan, a Maasai is from. There are actually ten subtribes, or clans, of Maasai who speak different dialects of the Maa language. The differences in subtribes might not be obvious to a visitor, but the Maasai can distinguish between the subtribes with no difficulty. There has, sadly, been a history of fighting between some of the clans, and this hostility has in the past affected the spread of the gospel among them.

Maasai and their cows

To understand the Maasai is to understand their relationship to their herd animals—cows, goats, and sheep. Cattle, however, have a special place in Maasai life. The number of cattle a man owns is a reflection of his wealth and status. Even babies' lives are influenced by cattle. The Maasai proverb, "A baby girl means beautiful cows," refers to the bride price paid by the groom to the girl's father, a price usually paid in cattle. The intertwined relationship of family and animals is reflected in another Maasai proverb about what a successful man needs: "a wife, a cow, a sheep, a goat, and a donkey."

Maasai exist on a diet mainly of cow's blood mixed with milk. Their daily lives revolve around livestock chores—milking, herding, caring for the young, finding pasture and water. Losing a herd would not be just a financial hardship for a Maasai—it would be a catastrophe on many levels. And in recent years, Maasai have experienced that kind of a catastrophe due to a drought much more severe than the drought recently experienced in parts of the US. To keep from losing their herds, and thus their whole livelihood, many Maasai have had to relocate, walking up to 60 or 80 miles away to places where they have heard water is available. Many times they walk long distances because a sprinkling of water has fallen in that

area. Some animals can keep up the pace of the forced drives—others cannot and succumb to weakness, predators, and heat.

At one time the Maasai had many square miles of grassland to roam freely with their herds. Now with Nairobi's city limits sprawling outward and other land being designated as national preserves and parks, the Maasai find themselves increasingly hemmed in. The government is pressuring the Maasai to mark off land as belonging to individuals. The modern world is closing in on the traditional world of the Maasai. Some Maasai have seen it coming and tried to prepare, others want to fight change all the way. There is little hope that fighting these cultural and political changes would be any more successful than the Maasai's fight against the British in the last century.

Maasai Christian leaders see God using these cultural and physical changes to reach their people. A Maasai pastor named Richard explained it this way:

8

"The Holy Spirit is really opening the door to the Maasai. When God is working, we will come to Christ. The Maasai are seeing a lot of changes. At one time, [we] depended on cattle alone. . . . Land is almost gone, cattle are being lost in drought, . . . so a lot of changes and a lot of needs. . . . We are seeing God meet these needs."

Boys and girls

The Maasai love their children, as do parents everywhere. They value family and having many children is a sign of an abundant life. In Maasai culture, families work together taking care of the all-important herds.

Boys and girls are considered children until about the age of 14, when they undergo rites of passage into adulthood. Before that age, they tend the herds of goats and stay at home helping their mothers. Maasai children love to run and sing. They even sing while tending the herds.

They play with homemade toys, since they must make their own entertainment. Like children everywhere, they like to climb trees.

Gender roles are well defined. Girls milk the cows and goats as well as tend the herds. They also watch their younger siblings, training for their own roles as mothers. They are expected to tackle multiple tasks. It is not uncommon to see an 8-year-old girl, baby brother or sister strapped to her back, herding goats along the dusty grasslands.

While girls handle such domestic chores, boys also tend the goats. They may walk a long way to find grass and water for the animals, and they learn to defend them from fierce predators. Their tasks are much like that of David during his days as a shepherd boy. These young

Maasai know the day will soon come when they become *morani,* or warriors.

These are the traditional roles of Maasai children, and for now they are still the norm. School is now a reality for many Maasai, however. While many schools are available, the family must pay tuition, so it is usually the oldest son who receives an education. When he returns home from his schoolday, he shares what he learned with his younger siblings.

To attend high school, the student must pass an entrance exam. High school is very expensive and not many students from the elementary schools can afford more schooling, even if they pass the exam. After high school, students must pass another test to be considered for university education.

Though it is expensive, more Maasai are seeing the necessity of education for their children. Twenty years ago when some young Maasai chose education over the more traditional life of the morani, they were criticized and laughed at. Now these mature young men, many of whom are Christians, are seen as leaders among their people. Missionary David Crane points out, "They are seen as the ones who can lead the Maasai into the changes that they must make if they are to keep their tribe intact. The Maasai as a whole are now beginning to see that they cannot continue to live as if the rest of the world does not exist.

"The modern world has come to them, whether they like it or not; and the forces of change that have come with the world are placing their culture in a state of flux. Thus the younger men that Baptists have typically worked with since the early 1980s are well positioned to use their influence in their community for the cause of Christ."

Dress
At one time the Maasai wore animal skins; now, only a few remote groups still wear skins. Others have switched

to the red plaid *shukas,* or blanket-type clothing they wear draped across their long, lean bodies. Their relationship to their cattle also affects the way Maasai dress. Shepherds carry long sharp spears and short swords to protect their animals against roving lions, leopards, and hyenas.

Some Maasai pastors have adopted Western dress such as suits and ties. They do not see this as any betrayal of their identity as Maasai. As one pastor pointed out, Maasai had not always worn shukas. It became the style to wear them, so they feel free to adopt another style, in this case Western clothing, if they see fit.

Homes

Maasai share their world with a host of wild animals, many of which would love to feast on Maasai cattle and goats. To protect their herds and themselves, Maasai build thorn fences around their villages. (These are not brier-type thorns such as Americans would know, but thorns big and sharp enough to flatten a car tire.) Indoor plumbing, running water, and electricity are unthinkable luxuries to the typical Maasai. The life of all Maasai, but particularly wives and mothers, is dictated by the need for two resources: water and firewood.

Maasai women

"Man works from sun to sun, but woman's work is never done." Maasai women would probably agree with this old saying. At no time is a Maasai woman's workload easy, but drought has made daily life much harder. During the drought season, a woman gets up early to wait in line at the water hole. Each family gets a turn, which might come as early as 2:00 A.M. If the woman misses her turn, her family and cows will have no water that day.

At daylight she milks the cows and sends them out, where the men or children will drive them along to grass and water, if it can be found. The woman then makes tea and sends her school-aged children off to begin their day. By now it is only about 6:00 A.M. School starts at 7:30 and most children live at least an hour's walk from school.

The woman then continues to look for water; she may walk up to 13 kilometers (8 miles) to find water. She must also gather firewood, and, as trees are scarce in the grass-lands, this can take a long time. If she has found water and fire-wood by the afternoon, she can use that time to clean up and do chores such as washing clothes. Laundry time is a time to socialize with other women.

During all these tasks, she is also taking care of her babies, those children too young for school or herding chores. If she or one of her children is sick, she may take them to a clinic such as the one operated by missionary Renee Crane. Besides receiving health care, she can visit with Renee or other Maasai women at the clinic.

If it is a Friday, the mother will go to market to buy supplies for the family for the coming week.

Every day at dark she prepares the one meal of the day, which is usually *ugali* (boiled cornmeal) and milk.

Sometimes she can add *sukuma* (greens) or beans. After the meal the mother looks after the herds which have been brought in from pasture. She does a head count of the animals and tends the goats. The youngest goats she brings into the house for the night. She then milks the cows again before her workday ends.

Cow rolling—a matter of prayer

Caring for livestock requires unceasing vigilance. Even in good times they must be guided and protected. In drought times, life revolves even more around the needs of the cows. During a drought the cows weaken; their joints grow sore. Understandably, the cows want to lie down at night. If they lie down for more than about two hours, however, the cows become very sick and could die. So in addition to her other duties, the Maasai woman has to get up and make the cows move every two hours. If the cow does not feel like getting up, rolling it to its feet or picking it up can be a backbreaking chore.

Many times when the drought was at its worst missionaries would stop to help roll cows. Renee Crane treated many Maasai for shoulder, back, and arm pain caused by repetitive cow moving. She wrote: "Every time I wake up I pray for the women picking up the cows. It's amazing but those prayers work. For exam-ple, the pastor's wife didn't lose a cow—most Maasai lost half their herds, but she didn't lose a single one. That's a miracle—those cows are really heavy."

Maasai men

The typical job of a Maasai man is to look after his cattle from morning until evening. In the past few years it has been very hard to find enough water for the cattle, and he may have to walk long distances to find enough to sustain them. He may end up digging in a dry creek bed hoping to find water just under the soil. The cows may end up having to go two or three days without water. Sometimes men have no food to take with them, only a cup of tea to nourish them.

The peer group that a Maasai boy grows up with remains important to him his whole life. Boys of the same age are circumcised together when they reach about 14 years old. After that they are considered men.

Age groupings, called age sets, dominate the pattern of Maasai life. A man forever identifies with the other young men in his age set. Those who are circumcised together are part of an age set. This social grouping is a big advantage to Maasai evangelists and church planters. Where a missionary might be met with suspicion or polite hospitality, a Maasai Christian of the same age set will be recognized as one of them, and his words given more weight. He can also be assured when he enters a village he will find a welcome from men in his age set.

MAASAI WORDS

Maasai [MAH-sigh]: name of the Maasai people, meaning "Maa-speaking people."

Maa [Mah]: language of the Maasai.

Boma [bow-mah]: Swahili term for cluster of Maasai homes.

Enkang' [ehn-KAHNG]: cluster of Maasai homes.

Morani [more-AHN-ee]: men between the ages of about 14 and 30, who form the warrior class.

Ilmorani [ill-more-AHN-ee]: young men between the ages of 13 and 20, who are the warriors—not really a class, but a stage of the Maasai life; i.e., child. This term covers everything before a warrior because he has not been circumcised, junior warrior, senior warrior, junior elder, senior elder.

Keji Enkarna Ai [KAY-gee ehn-CAR-nah eye] _____. : My name is *(fill in name)*.

Kara olairukoni [CAHR-a oh-lie-roo-CO-knee]: I am a Christian.

Tenkaraki atajeuo [Tan-CAH-rah-key ah-tay-JAY-oh]: Because I am saved.

Ainguaa Amerika [ang-WAAH ah-may-REE-kah]: I come from America.

Kashipa taata atii ene [kah-SHEE-pah TAAH-tah ah-TEE EH-nay]: I am happy to be here.

Atishipe oleng [ah tee-SHEE-pay oh-LEHNG]: I am very happy.

Mesisi Yesu [MEH-see-see YEAH-sue]: Praise the Lord.

Enkai Supat [ehn-ka-EE SOU-pot]: Supreme God.

Boy's names

Muia [Moy-yah]

Saruni [Sah-roo-ny]

Girl's names:

Nasarian [Nah-sah-ry-ahn]

Kaswii [Kah-swy]

2

TODAY'S MISSIONARY AMONG THE MAASAI

If God calls you to be a missionary, don't stoop to be a king.—Jordan Grooms

In some ways missionary life among the Maasai fulfills the classic idea of a missionary—someone who lives in the bush amidst physical hardship and social isolation, sharing the gospel with a tribal people. But that's hardly the whole picture. The Southern Baptist missionaries among the Maasai face specific challenges in the bush. Conveniences such as water, electricity, and telephones are rare or nonexistent. Life can be hard and lonely. It can also be filled with joy and satisfaction as they work alongside Maasai Christians to give all Maasai the opportunity to respond to the gospel. Unlike some of their missionary predecessors from other centuries, today's missionaries have not come to spread Western culture, but to present the New Testament gospel while modeling a New Testament type of church.

This chapter profiles some current missionaries to the Maasai and provides a brief look at their daily lives in Africa. Notice it is a look at their daily lives, but not a look at a "typical" day, for as one mission-ary pointed out, "There is no typical day in the bush." Missionaries do not keep office hours or even regular visit-ing hours. Every day can bring a new problem in the guise of sickness or a flat tire or a cow that can't stand up. Every day can bring new opportunities in the shape of visitors or requests for help at a new church. The Maasai team of missionaries faces a delicate balancing act: How much time should they spend traveling? How much time should they give to training new church leaders? What resources do they have to share with Maasai who are sick or injured? What should they do about their children's edu-cation? When is there enough time for their own spiritual growth and physical rest?

The missionaries need and want the prayers of other Christians as they make choices and respond to the pres-sures of circumstances and opportunities.

Making a home in the bush

While a house by itself is not a home, it is hard to have a home without some kind of house to live in. The mission-aries have faced the question of where to live, and several have built their own homes or had them built. Earlier mis-sionaries had to build their own homes, so missionary husbands needed to be handy at all kinds of construction. Now the East Africa Region of the International Mission Board (IMB) has a missionary, Dennis Maupin, who helps bush missionaries build their homes. He assisted the Moors of Tanzania and the Cranes of Kenya in building their homes so they could keep focusing on church plant-ing among the Maasai. Still, questions exist related to finding and transporting needed materials, finding local builders to help with the work, and, always, the question of access to water.

The Cranes have the newest missionary house in Kenya. It is located on Oloitokitok [oh-low-ee-TOE-key-talk] Road, which runs between the Mombasa-Nairobi Highway and the town of Oloitokitok, which in turn is located at the base of Mount Kilimanjaro. (Mount Kilimanjaro is the highest peak in Africa and one of the most majestic mountains in the world.) This is an unforgettable setting for a home. But the Cranes chose their home site because of the presence of an old borehole. The actual name of their home site is *Oltinka loonkaik* (meaning "hand pump" in Maasai). The borehole had only a hand pump for many years. The Mission fixed the borehole and added an electric pump. Using electricity from their 10,000-watt generator, the Cranes are able to pump water into their home.

David and Joy Cox do not have the benefit of a well near their home. Dependent on rainwater (which can be very scarce in Maasailand), the Coxes have learned how to use water with maximum efficiency. Their rain gutters carry water to large cisterns where it is stored. When drought hits their area, the Coxes have to buy water, which is brought to their house from a source like a river.

Security is as big a concern to the missionaries as is water, but it is more of an issue in some places than in others. All the missionaries own dogs that can bark a warning if robbers threaten. For example, the Cox family has two German shepherds named Tuffy and Lobo, as well as a high-spirited Jack Russell terrier named Sammy.

David Cox was appointed as a missionary to eastern Africa in June 1998, along with his wife, Joy Cox. A native of Raleigh, North Carolina, David graduated from North Carolina State University and Southeastern Baptist Theological Seminary, also in North Carolina.

Joy Floyd Cox was

born in Lumberton, North Carolina, and calls Fairmont her hometown. She earned an associate degree in nursing from Wake Technical Community College in Raleigh and attended the University of North Carolina at Chapel Hill. Before becoming a missionary, Joy worked as a nurse in Raleigh. They have two sons, Micah David, born in 1991; and John Caleb, born in 1992. David and Joy served in Kenya through the IMB's International Service Corps before their current assignment.

All the missionaries have night guards who patrol their compounds. The road the Cranes live on has a reputation for being a popular route with smugglers. Robberies and carjackings occur there frequently. Rob Kopesky and his family were robbed not far from the Cranes' home, and Rob was left with eight titanium plates and 32 screws in his face.

"That is not the sort of experience they teach you about in seminary, but it is a part of the collective price that has been paid by missionaries to take the gospel to the Maasai people," wrote David Crane.

Travel

Most of the Kenya missionary team drive approximately 40,000 kilometers (approximately 25,000 miles) per year. Maasailand is a huge region and churches sprawl across the area. The plentiful thorn trees act as a natural booby trap for car tires. A missionary can have up to 40 flat tires in a year, and does not have the luxury of an auto club or tow truck to come to the rescue. Missionary wives and even children become handy at changing flats.

A four-wheel-drive vehicle is essential in Maasailand. Not only are the roads rough in dry weather, but when the heavy rains do come, roads become muddy to the point of impassability. Missionaries can easily become mired in mud or in flooded-out creek beds.

Besides the risk of accident, breakdown, or weather hazard, travel is dangerous for its overall effect on the body. The dust flies up along the dry dirt roads stinging eyes, filling lungs, and causing respiratory trouble. During droughts the dust can become unbearable. New vehicles have air-conditioning. Older missionary transportation did not have air-conditioning. Betty Cummins and Peggy Hooten had to leave Maasai areas due to lung problems inflicted by dust. The cost of an air-conditioned car is small compared to the cost of having a missionary leave the area.

The rutted unpaved roads are the cause of many back and neck injuries among missionaries. If you have ever jolted along an unpaved road, you know the impact it can have on your body. Try to imagine the results of thousands of miles of such travel. Or, you could ask Renee Crane.

From December 1993 to March 1998 the Cranes drove a double cab Toyota Hilux, an extremely tough vehicle that can make it through almost any road conditions. However, a smooth ride is not one of its good points, even on the small number of paved roads in the Cranes' work area. On the dirt roads, the constant riding in the Hilux was a bone-jarring experience. Several missionaries ended up with back and neck problems, including David's wife, Renee.

In July 1997 the rough traveling took its toll on a disk in her back, which herniated. She spent a week in Nairobi Hospital. During that stay, her doctors realized she needed an operation to prevent permanent damage to nerves in her leg. She not only had to fly back to the US for the surgery, she had to lie flat during the flight, which meant she had to travel first-class on British Airways in order to have a seat that reclined flat. The whole Crane family flew to the US for two months of medical leave.

After what seemed a complete recovery, the next year the problem flared again, and doctors feared Renee needed a second operation. After an exam by her

Robert "Bob" Calvert is the team leader for the Maasai missionaries. He and his wife, Nancy, were appointed to eastern Africa in July 1990. He was born in Little Rock, Arkansas, and graduated from University of Central Arkansas and Southwestern Baptist Theological Seminary. Before his current assignment as church developer in Kenya, Bob served on several church staffs, and still uses his hobbies of singing and playing guitar in his current role. Given the Maasai love of music, he uses this talent a lot on the missions field in Kenya.

Nancy Felts Calvert is from Atlanta, Georgia. She is a registered nurse, with a master of divinity degree from Southwestern Baptist Theological Seminary. Before her assignment as a church and home worker in Kenya, Nancy was a nurse in Atlanta and Fort Worth. Their children are Christine Rose, born in 1985; Abigail Deborah, born in 1988; Robert Thomas, born in 1990; and Zachary Andrew, born in 1992.

David and Renee Crane were appointed to eastern Africa in April 1993. Born in El Paso, Texas, David considers Cherryville, North Carolina, his hometown. David earned a degree from Columbia (S.C.) Bible College and Seminary and also graduated from Southeastern Baptist Theological Seminary in Wake Forest.

Before his current assignment as church developer among the Maasai, David was a church staff member. His love of camping has come to good use in his work in Maasailand.

Renee Adams Crane, born in Lincolnton, North Carolina, also considers Cherryville her hometown. A registered nurse, she is the mother of Thomas Scott, born in 1980; Zebulon Howard, born in 1984; and Mary Catherine, born in 1986.

Renee continues to use her nursing skills in her role as church and home worker among the Maasai.

American physicians, she learned an operation was not necessary. This was good news. In order to avoid such problems in the future, however, Renee would have to be very careful. She must make her traveling choices wisely, and often use anti-inflammatory drugs to prevent swelling in the damaged disk. All this because of the type of travel missionaries to the Maasai must do.

In order to prevent more of such injuries, the Mission has purchased an expensive four-wheel-drive vehicle that also provides a comfortable ride and still allows missionaries to travel wherever they need to go. In addition to the initial expense of the vehicle, the import tax of 100 percent in Kenya doubles the cost.

"We all want to thank Southern Baptists for their generous giving to the Lottie Moon Christmas Offering because that makes it possible for us to buy the sort of comfortable four-wheel-drive vehicles which can, on the one hand, enable us to travel anywhere in Maasailand, and, on the other hand, do so at a level of comfort that does not endanger our backs," said David Crane.

Family life

Caring for the needs of children is a big part of missionary family life. A big question is, How will we educate our children? While school is becoming more common among the Maasai people, they are few and far between in the undeveloped areas. Existing schools are not of the best quality. Most of the Maasai missionaries have two options: homeschool or boarding school. The Rift Valley Academy, located in Kijabe, Kenya, is an Africa Inland Mission-sponsored boarding school many missionaries use. Boarding school allows missionaries' kids opportunities to get to know other American young people and to participate in typical school activities such as sports. The separation between children and parents, however, is hard on everyone, as borne out by Renee Crane in this journal entry.

"Zeb and Thomas being away at school has been one of the hardest things I have experienced. I miss them so much. I still am not convinced that this is the best thing. Our options at this point are few. They really do not want to homeschool, which at this time is the only other alternative. They seem to be happy, but I know they miss family and home."

Homeschooling keeps the family together and is a popular option for families with younger children, but it is a task that falls to the missionary wife and mother, and consumes a large part of her day. This fact, in turn, limits the ministry she can have outside the home. A mother who spends the bulk of her day teaching her own children and caring for the home faces loneliness and isolation. And while children can receive an excellent education in a homeschool setting, they do not have as many traditional school experiences such as team sports, clubs, and other activities.

The Calvert family, who lives close to Nairobi, is fortunate to have a third option, that of using a day school called Rosslynn Academy, partially sponsored by the IMB. But this option requires a lot of traveling back and forth by the Calvert parents and their children.

No matter what educational choice a family makes, it affects the rest of their family life, and cannot be made lightly. However, like any family, missionary families do not sit around all the time grappling with weighty issues. They go to church, do household chores, enjoy their pets, have personal Bible study and prayer, and they have fun. Building in fun times is an important way to fight the loneliness that can set in, and it is a kind of fun few families in the world enjoy, set in the outdoors of Africa.

Maasailand is home to some of the world's finest wild animal game parks. Missionaries frequently take their kids camping in these parks, and exotic animals such as elephants, giraffes, lions, and rhinos are familiar sights to the missionaries' kids. The Cranes have also climbed on Mount Kilimanjaro and Mount Kenya. The Coxes enjoy camping and spending time at Lake Naivasha, about an hour from their home.

Families also enjoy more traditional pastimes: the Coxes might spend a family night that involves playing board games and watching videos, or traveling to Nairobi for pizza and ice cream. Micah and Caleb enjoy playing with their dogs, as well as their dwarf hamsters and pet chameleons.

Older missionaries' children like to ride motorcycles through the invitingly open spaces of the bush. Besides the freedom and fun the motorcycle offers, it gives the rider a chance to surprise the busloads of tourists who come out to look at big game animals. As tourists on the buses ooh and aah over their exotic surroundings, their eyes widen and mouths drop open at the sight of an Anglo teenager zipping by on a motorcycle, waving gleefully!

Life of the missionary wife

Each missionary wife has her own set of duties and responsibilities based on the ages of her children, needs of her family, her gifts, and her own sense of calling. Joy Cox homeschools her sons, keeps the home, helps the Maasai who come to their house looking for help, and studies the Maa language.

Renee Crane is a nurse and has found many ways to use her medical skills among the Maasai. But, her medical ministry takes place in the larger context of her missionary calling and her life in Africa. She operates a clinic from her home, located at the foot of snowy Mount Kilimanjaro.

Renee starts off her day with Bible study, by herself or with a group. She organizes the day. Will she be working with a team of volunteers? Is there a Maasai association meeting? The answers to these questions help shape her day.

Her major goal of the day is to get everyone out the door, headed in the right direction. She starts her high school-aged daughter Mary on her schoolwork. Son Zeb is in boarding school, and Thomas is in college in the US. Renee then helps Margaret, her Maasai worker, do whatever needs to be done in the house.

Renee tries to provide hospitality to their many visitors. It is rare for the Cranes to have a meal by themselves, and visitors are in and out of the house constantly. "We are closer to many here than you would ever believe. Our Maasai neighbors are our Kenyan family."

Clinic ministry

Renee tries to be in the medical clinic by 11:30 A.M. in order to see as many patients as possible. She works on a first-come, first-served basis. If the patient is a Christian, she prays with that fellow believer. If the patient is not a Christian, she shares her faith with that person. Some people have become Christians while visiting the clinic.

During one epidemic of intestinal virus, Renee and her Maasai friend Margaret kept the clinic open several hours a day. Renee was grateful for the medicines some volunteers had left behind. They came in handy when treating Maasai children with high fevers and swollen tonsils.

For several reasons, Renee dispensed medicine at her home clinic rather than sending medicine home with the

Maasai mothers. This required that mothers bring their children to Renee's home every day for treatment, but it was necessary. Refrigerated medicines must stay with the Cranes, for they have a refrigerator and the Maasai do not. Also, Renee has the medical training required to understand the seven-to-ten-day regimen for giving medicine, and the Maasai mothers do not. Whenever their children cry, they want to give the medicine. Renee cannot even send cough syrup home with the families, for some older Maasai are likely to drink it as an alcoholic beverage.

Through her clinic ministry Renee continually learns more about Maasai culture and ways of doing things. Renee recalls one patient: "One 13-year-old girl came in and I was unable to see the back of her throat or the uvula. Her tongue was bleeding too, and she was extremely thin, weak, and sick looking. I could not get her off my mind the rest of the day. I have since learned that a bleeding tongue is a sign of malnutrition and that the Maasai cut out the uvula if someone is coughing too much. They believe that if you cough a lot, the uvula will grow long and hang down in your throat and choke you to death. So they just cut it out."

Besides delivering babies, teaching health, and nursing the sick and injured, Renee has come into contact with the health concerns caused by the Maasai custom of female circumcision. This practice occurs in many parts of Africa and the Middle East in many people groups of various religious backgrounds. Sometimes it is practiced on infants, sometimes on children. Among the Maasai, it happens when a girl is about 14 years old.

Female circumcision refers to the cutting away of part or all of the female genitals. This is supposed to prepare a girl for marriage. The consequences of this circumcision can be infection of the wound, spread of HIV, and scarring that interferes with childbirth. Many political and human rights groups have objected to this practice, but it continues.[1]

The clinic has given Renee a window into the lives of Maasai women. She sees how they can suffer from spouse abuse, from typhoid and intestinal worms carried in dirty water, from back problems created by long years of carrying water and firewood. It has also given her the chance to model Christ's love for them.

"My experiences are stretching my nursing skills, but I am enjoying it. Each person that comes through the clinic is prayed for and talked to about Jesus," Renee says.

[1] For more information about female genital mutilation, visit this Web site: www.fgm.org. It contains helpful information and numerous links to other related sites. While this site is not Christian in nature or purpose, it does contain much information Christians need in order to respond in Christlike compassion and advocacy to this issue. Be aware that the information on these sites can be disturbing and is in no way suitable for children.

3

HISTORY OF MISSIONS WORK AMONG THE MAASAI

When God decides to begin drawing a people group to Himself, there is no one in heaven or earth who will be able to stop Him.—David Crane, missionary to the Maasai

A recent newspaper article described a North American affliction called "same day syndrome." Symptoms include impatience with waiting and a need for immediate gratification. A missionary to the Maasai suffering from same day syndrome would not last very long. The Maasai have a strong cultural identity and have long been resistant to the gospel. Work among them has been slow but faithful. Today's hardworking missionaries recognize the efforts of those who have sown seeds long before they arrived. As David Crane said, "When God decides to begin drawing a people group to Himself, there is no one in heaven or earth who will be able to stop Him, and those early Maasai missionaries launched out with those sorts of convictions. Like trailblazers in other fields of endeavor, the fruits of their efforts were to become more apparent after they were gone from the stage."

Following is a brief synopsis of the missions efforts that led to the work with Maasai today.

1973

John and Kathy Dillman became the first IMB missionaries to be involved with the Maasai. They worked with some Africa Inland Mission (AIM) missionaries in Kajiado District helping with a feeding project among the Maasai. A drought had ravaged that part of Kenya, and the feeding project was a way to show Christian love and concern to the Maasai. Later on Carl and Gerry Hall, also IMB missionaries, became involved with this relief food effort. This yearlong feeding project touched Maasai in 32 villages. As a result of this work, 200 Maasai received Christ; literacy classes, Bible studies, and nutrition classes were begun; and the Halls and Dillmans were called into working with the Maasai full-time.

1975

The Dillmans relocated to the Loita Hills of Narok District, known for the Maasai Mara Game Reserve. For six years they focused on various ministries to help meet medical and literacy needs as well as on evangelism. The Dillmans learned to speak Maasai very well, and tried to live very simply, as much like the Maasai as possible. Their work led others to come and share their ministry in the Narok District.

1976

This year saw the start of a preaching point that had been a matter of great prayer for IMB missionaries Harold and Betty Cummins. This couple had lived on the edge of Maasailand as they worked with the Wakamba people. Their rented house was part of the Wilson Ranch situated near the Mombasa-Nairobi Highway. The highway forms a boundary between the Maasai and Wakamba areas. The

Cumminses would literally look over into Maasai country and pray for God to open a door for them to work with the Maasai. The door opened with the help of a ranch guard named Bernard Leitengangi.

Bernard was not Maasai, but Samburu. After he became a Christian, however, he felt a burden to share the gospel with the Maasai. This was more possible for Bernard than it would have been for some Africans because the Samburu share many cultural similarities with the Maasai, and their languages are very similar. When Bernard shared his feelings with Harold, the missionary was thrilled to help him. Because of the realities of Maasai culture, Harold advised Bernard to focus on leading men to Christ before women and children. This strategy was not an insinuation that the souls of women and children were less important than the souls of men, but an acknowledgement that in Maasai culture, men are seen as the decision makers. In reality, the men spend many nights in their homes discussing an important matter with Maasai women and listening to the women's opinions before making a final decision. But, they want important decisions presented to them.

A preaching point was begun near Ilmamen, where the presence of a new school indicated the people's openness to new ideas. Although the advice was to focus on men converts, women and children mainly came for worship. When a leader named Simon Kaipoon emerged, a baptismal service for 38 people was held, and the Ilmamen Baptist Church was born. After this, Bernard simply disappeared. Years later an Ilmamen elder recounted the story that some Maasai men who resented the spread of the gospel knowingly brought false charges of adultery against Bernard. He apparently left the area after this. Still, the work he did remained and bore fruit, and he is counted among the trailblazers of Christian work with the Maasai. These early workers did not have all the answers to work with the Maasai when they started. They relied on prayer and their sense of urgency from God to reach the Maasai. They went through the open doors they found at the time. Could they have done better or differently? Perhaps. But if they had waited until there was no risk of failure, the Maasai might still be waiting to hear the gospel.

Also this year, the Halls moved to the Matapao area of Maasailand and started the Engaboli Farming Scheme Project. This was a model farm begun among the Maasai, with the hope that teaching them farming techniques would help them avoid famine in the future. In 1985 their farm project was closed. Four churches were started in Matapao during this time.

1983

By this time Harold Cummins was spending half his time working with the Maasai. Wakamba Christians were his co-workers. The Wakambas and Maasai were old enemies. Though the last war between them ended in 1963, many Maasai men who had fought in that war had not forgiven or forgotten it. Since Wakambas and Maasai had been mortal enemies for many years, Harold and his co-workers knew they could not stay in Maasailand after the sun went down; that would have been a foolish risk. Already the Wakamba Christians were risking their safety to make sure their old enemies had the chance to become their new brothers in Christ. Also by 1983, Harold's work in Kaputiei had grown to 6 churches. Maasai leaders were essential to the growth and strength of the churches, so Harold invested himself in training younger Maasai men through a method called Theological Education by Extension (TEE). This method used books for training, and younger men were more likely than the older men to be literate. Time has proven the good thinking of this approach, since many of those young men Harold trained have continued as mature leaders of Kaputiei Association's churches.

1986

Through the combination of leader training, evangelism, and church starts, Harold's area had 16 churches by 1986. That was also the year that an annual meeting for women and children began. The youth meeting featured a choir competition, which sparked interest in developing choirs in the churches and in writing hymns and choruses in the Maasai language. The importance of music development in starting African churches cannot be underestimated. "Music is a vital part of all African cultures; and no movement will go far among any group of Africans that does not utilize music and singing," observed David Crane.

Also in 1986, Peggy and Jim Hooten transferred to Kenya from Uganda in order to work full-time in Kaputiei. They also worked in Matapato, as the Halls had left the area. Like the Cumminses and the Halls, the Hootens were already veteran missionaries before they began work with the Maasai.

1987–88

A major chapter in Maasai work was written in 1987–88 with the launch of the Maasai Evangelism Project (MEP). During the MEP, evangelists from the Kaputiei Association went into areas of Suswa, Matapato, and Magadi/Ngong. The special significance of this was that the Kaputiei Maasai were reaching Maasai of different clans. (See chap. 1 for information about the hostility between different clans, or subtribes, of Maasai.) In Magadi/Ngong the MEP was based on five months of survey work and relationship building done by Harold Cummins. He had visited in scores of homes. There were already three Bible studies started at the time the MEP was launched. The MEP resulted in 7 churches with 200 baptized members. Evangelism teams also went into Oloitokitok and Suswa. A Kenyan Baptist home missionary and Christians from the Kisongo Maasai clan had already done work there. Because of bad feelings between the Kauptiei and Kisongo Maasai, however, this work ended. Many new churches and preaching points were begun through the MEP and ministries such as literacy workshops and medical clinics. Results were mixed. *The COMMISSION* magazine noted, "There was some success and some failure. The evangelists were driven violently from some areas."

Harold Cummins later observed that the rapid rate of evangelistic effort had to be slowed to allow more time for training and discipleship and more careful church planting. The goal of the MEP was not to garner short-term results, but to plant the gospel in healthy, biblically based churches that could reproduce.

The missionaries and Maasai Christians learned a great deal from the 1987–88 MEP and applied the experience to the 1992–94 MEP.

1988

Herb and Becky Cady moved to Narok to work in Suswa. The Cadys did not leave Suswa until 1996. During those eight years Herb worked on a water project to benefit many Maasai. (Herb also started a Baptist Leaders Training School which in 1997 became a Bible school which graduated its first class of students in November 1999.) The number of churches in the Narok district rose to 30, but then dropped between 1991 and 1993. Again, intertribal warfare took a toll on the progress of sharing the gospel. More churches closed after the Cadys' departure, but 6 new congregations began during the first year David and Joy Cox worked in Suswa.

1989

Bruce and Martha Schmidt located in the Matapato area. A Bible school was begun. In his first four-year term with the Maasai, Bruce saw 650 people become Christians. By 1993, when a new MEP was launched, 600 to 800 people a month in his area became Christians.

1990

Bob and Nancy Calvert, current missionaries to the Maasai, were appointed to Eastern Africa.

1992

Maa translation of the Bible was finished. (The New Testament had been completed years earlier.)

1992–94

The MEP during these years depended much more on Maasai evangelists going into homes and witnessing one-on-one. When foreign visitors offer an invitation after a gospel presentation, Africans are likely to respond out of politeness. If the visitor wants them to say they accept Jesus, they likely will say yes out of politeness—it seems to mean so much to the visitor. When Maasai present the gospel to other Maasai, numbers of conversions are far more likely to be accurate.

1993

David Crane became church developer for Kaputiei. He and Maasai leaders and churches developed several new churches based on the work done during the 1992–94 MEP.

1998

David and Joy Cox were appointed to the Maasai team of missionaries.

Linking the past and present

In 2001 three Southern Baptist career missionary couples work full-time with the Maasai in Kenya: Bob and Nancy Calvert, David and Joy Cox, and David and Renee Crane. Their Tanzanian counterparts—Tim and Ann Tidenberg and Rob and Lisa Moor—also work with Maasai there, as this people group stretches beyond the borders of one country. Church planting continued to thrive in the 1990s. The next chapters reveal the work God is doing among the Maasai today and what the future may hold for them.

IMB missionary Bob Calvert with a group of Maasai evangelists who live in tents two weeks a month on the plains and spend their days in going village to village sharing the gospel with other Maasai. Calvert is teaching them to become church leaders and eventually take his place.

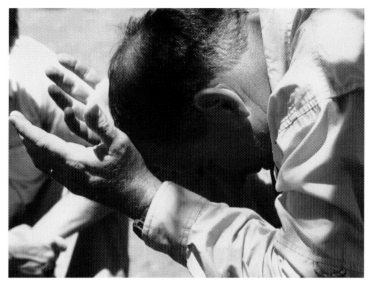

IMB missionary Bob Calvert prays with a man who is receiving Christ.

IMB missionary Renee Crane checks people in the health clinic where she is a nurse practitioner. The woman in red is her nursing assistant. Crane is a missionary to the Maasai in Kenya.

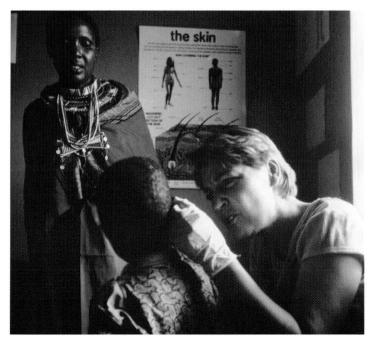

Tim Tidenberg talks with Lazaro O'pusongu, pastor of the Gelai Baptist Church. Photo taken in Lazaro's village of Lumbwa.

A group of Maasai look on as Ann Tidenberg treats a small child of his wounds in the village of Lumbwa. Ann receives a large amount of basic medical supplies from the states to treat minor wounds in the villages they visit.

4

CHURCH PLANTING BY AND WITH THE MAASAI

Let the Maasai be the Maasai.—Bob Calvert, missionary to the Maasai

---

Christianity has not come to the Maasai in a spiritual vacuum. The traditional Maasai religion is monotheistic—it embraces belief in one God, Enkai, whom they fear and worship. In the Maasai community, however, worship and sacrifices are offered to God on special occasions. The community's advocate with Enkai is the *Olioboni,* who takes the role of seer, prophet, healer, or shaman. This man wields great influence in the lives of young Maasai men, as this chapter will reveal later.

Maasai religion has no tradition of a personal relationship with God as Christians have through Jesus Christ. Maasai elders tell stories to the children which they believe were legends handed down by their ancestors, but which resonate with many Old Testament teachings. Missionaries bringing the gospel emphasize Jesus' identity as the Son of God.

The age set system mentioned in chapter 1 is affected by the traditional religion. When young men reach the age of 13 to 14 years old, older Maasai men circumcise them. They then undergo a period of training by fire stick elders (men two age sets above the boys being trained). Boys learn how to use weapons in warfare and cattle raids. During this time they take part in certain ceremonies related to becoming a *morani* (warrior). The Olioboni blesses the young men as they undergo the rites of passage into manhood. This relationship with the Olioboni, whom one missionary called "the towering central figure in their culture" is one reason young Maasai Christian men shun the warrior system. They view the system as intertwined with the Maasai traditional religion, and allegiance to the Olioboni is seen as a major hurdle to Maasai men accepting the gospel.

Moreover, many practices the warrior tradition approves are incompatible with the Maasai understanding of Christianity. Morani like to prove their courage by lion hunts, a practice now against the law. There is much sexual activity outside of marriage. The warriors are encouraged to steal cattle in raids on neighboring tribes such as the Wakamba. Maasai Christian men wish to obey the laws of God and man.

The Maasai historically have fought hard to keep from being overwhelmed by outside forces, such as the British Empire. The warrior system has given them great power and caused other tribes to fear them. Because the warrior system has done so much to enhance Maasai power and been such an integral part of Maasai culture, many Maasai men want to keep it. These men have so far rejected Christianity rather than lose the warrior system. They do recognize, however, good aspects of Christianity, and for that reason many do allow their wives and children to attend church.

The warrior system can also help the spread of the gospel. Age mates (young men of the same age set, circumcised at the same time) are expected to offer hospitality to each other. A strong bond exists among these men, so strong that a Maasai pastor or evangelist can expect his age mates in any village to at least give him a hearing about the gospel. These Maasai Christians can spread the gospel in places where missionaries and American volunteers may have little hope of going.

Maasai worship services

Maasai Christians are not hampered by the need to have large church buildings—or any church building at all. Although most Maasai now live in permanent homes, few house churches exist. The church may meet under a tree, or, since trees are scarce, under a roof without walls. Benches are fashioned from handy materials like rocks, or wood suspended between rocks.

The church floor is dirt; and when the service gets under way, the dust flies under the feet of the worshipers as they literally jump for joy. ("You know it's been a good service if you come home dusty," one mission-ary observed.)

Lots of singing and clapping also marks Maasai worship services, with songs sung in the Maa language. Services are conducted in both Maasai and Kiswahili languages, and the bulk of the long services is worship. "The Maasai love to worship the Lord in music, song, and dance—they just want to worship," one missionary said.

As they do in every other aspect of Maasai life, cows even affect worship services. Church starts at 8:00 A.M.

with children's Sunday School, which lasts until 10:00. Then the children go home to watch the cows so their parents can come to church. Parents arrive about 11:00 A.M. for a service that may stretch to 2:00 or 3:00 in the afternoon.

"Worship is my favorite part. The different songs we sing, they draw me closer to the Lord. It is through our singing and dancing that we express ourselves," said a Maasai woman named Margaret.

Concerns about cows even come up during testimony time, a favorite part of the service. At one church a visitor arrived and explained that he had walked a long way looking for his straying cows. Hearing the vibrant singing in the church, he decided to stay. He asked for prayers to help find his cows. At the service's end he repeated his request. A friend of a church member ended up finding the missing cows. "Stuff like that happens all the time," one missionary noted.

Baptisms are a time of celebration in the Maasai church. The whole congregation walks to a water hole or river to witness the baptism, singing and clapping all the way. When the pastor immerses the convert, everyone is

quiet and reverent, but upon the believer's appearance from the water, fellow believers clap and sing with renewed joy.

Women dress in colorful clothes with many strands of beads for church services. They want to look their best. The beads are more than decoration—Maasai women wear beads to any very important occasion. In recent years, women have begun to wear their beads to their baptisms, signifying to all who see them how important their baptism is to them.

The Missionary's Role

The Maasai missionary team in Kenya has many responsibilities. They work with local churches to teach and promote evangelism and discipleship. They provide leadership training and help with church planting. For a church planting movement to grow, national Christians must be well discipled so they can in turn plant churches and disciple future generations of believers.

David and Joy Cox work with young churches that need help to grow. They also help plant churches in areas where no churches exist. Their area of work is far-reaching, with churches being as far as a 90-minute drive on the infamously bad roads. Many areas in their district have no churches at all yet. Numerous volunteer teams have come from the US to help the Coxes conduct animal clinics, medical clinics, construction projects, discipleship and leadership training, and evangelistic efforts.

"Worship is my favorite part. The different songs we sing, they draw me closer to the Lord. It is through our singing and dancing that we express ourselves."

The Coxes have been privileged to see God's power at work through the efforts of Maasai Christians, volunteers from the US, and their own work. During one visit from a volunteer group, some of the group members went with Maasai evangelists to preach the gospel to a family in a remote area where only a couple of churches existed at the time. Because outsiders did not frequent this area, the presence of volunteers frightened one old Maasai woman so badly she refused to leave her house. After a great deal of gentle coaxing, she stepped timidly outside. She listened to a wondrous message of a God Who loved her. She finally decided to accept Christ during that visit.

Later, David Cox and the Maasai evangelists returned
to the village for further teaching. This once shy woman
now stood up boldly and proudly recited a verse from the
Book of Mark. She radiated joy in her salvation and was
glad the Maasai Christians and American volunteers had
come to tell her about her Savior, Jesus Christ. Is it a surprise to know that a new church exists in that village
today?

While the younger Maasai men who have the benefit
of education are key to the spread of the gospel, it would
be a mistake, as the previous story shows, to think older
Maasai do not listen to the gospel. They have great influence over the spread of the gospel, as the following story
illustrates.

On another occasion, David Cox accompanied volunteers to a remote area devoid of roads or churches. While
some Maasai had heard the gospel, few had responded so
far. Elderly Maasai are especially difficult to witness to
since they have had a lifetime of trusting in other beliefs.
The day of this visit, David, a Maasai pastor, and two volunteers met two old men sitting on a tall hill outside the
village. The old men welcomed the group to their village.
One of the old men then left, but the other stayed and
gathered everyone in the village to hear about Jesus. After
the preaching and witnessing, several Maasai wanted to
accept Christ as Savior, including the old man who had
been their host. He could hardly wait to pray for Christ to
come into his life. Now this elderly man and his village
have heard the gospel and many have responded.

Storying the Bible

Both Maasai Christians and missionaries use a simple
method called chronological Bible storying (CBS) as part
of their strategy for reaching Maasai. The stories—over
100 of them in the Maa language—tell the Bible story
from Genesis to Jesus.

Storying is a popular and effective method of sharing the gospel and is used on many missions fields. When traveling to villages, Maasai evangelists sometimes take with them a series of cassette tapes and illustrated flip chart books called the "Look, Listen, and Learn" (LLL) series. They play cassettes on a hand-cranked tape player, which eliminates the need to have batteries or electricity. One Maasai cranks the tape player while another turns the pages of the large booklet to display pictures the story describes. Each story has several pictures. While the audience looks at the pictures, they listen to the story, and in so doing learn about God and His love for them.

The Maasai have responded enthusiastically to these stories. Two Maasai pastors, Jackson and John, have used the LLL method and report that people have asked to keep the materials so that they could listen to the stories again and again at night, inviting friends to come and enjoy the stories too. A village may typically keep a tape and book for a week, with the two pastors returning the next week with a new story, which is just as eagerly devoured by their waiting audience. From one village which used the tapes and books this way, a new church has started, all through the effect of stories!

As the church planting movement among the Maasai forms and grows, the missionaries are privileged to see Maasai Christians taking leadership roles in every area—as pastors, teachers, disciplers, evangelists. Pastors, evangelists, and lay leaders all work to start and grow new churches.

But, it is not yet time for the missionaries to leave the Maasai church. As David Cox said, "A premature exit may hinder a CPM (church planting movement) from moving into the final stage if converts and leaders are not properly developed and taught how to develop and train others."

Renee Crane echoed those feelings when she wrote, "We realize that we are not to the end of the work yet. We can see the end, but we are not there yet. We're here because we know without a shadow of a doubt, it's where God has us for now. . . . We know that we are to finish the vision God has given us to reach the Maasai with Christ and to train the leadership to take over completely."

Despite the hardships of life in the bush (one missionary wife compared it to pioneer life in the American frontier), the Maasai missionary team in Kenya appreciates working alongside the Maasai people. Joy Cox put it this way: "It is very easy to talk with Maasai about God and share about His love for them. It is a privilege to work among Maasai and to see a harvest of souls for the kingdom of God among these people in remote places of Kenya. Living in the bush, or countryside of Kenya, and working with Maasai is a pleasure because they are very loving to outsiders who care for them. We feel very welcomed and a part of their community."

Faithful in persecution

While the gospel is spreading through Maasailand, it is not free of resistance by those who do not wish to see it take root in Maasai hearts. While some Maasai men encourage their families to embrace Christianity, others abuse their wives for becoming Christian. These women face persecution within their own homes. Young men of the warrior age set who refuse to engage in some morani practices are ridiculed when they stand faithful. But some persecution goes beyond abuse and ridicule to the threat of death.

The following story, written by IMB missionary Sue Sprenkle, illustrates the dangers faced by the growing Maasai church and missionaries. These events took place in Tanzania, where Southern Baptist missionary Tim Tidenberg and his family serve.

Cries of "black blood or white blood" echoed through Maasailand as men grabbed clubs and spears in an effort to stop the spread of the gospel, which recently challenged parts of Maasai culture.

Christians in northern Tanzania went into hiding as large groups of Maasai morani (warriors) moved through villages, ransacking churches and threatening believers. International Mission Board missionary Tim Tidenberg's home became a sanctuary for local Christians of all denominations. After three weeks of destructive conflict, a resolution is in the works.

The Maasai are among the most colorful people in eastern Africa. Known for their bright red clothes and beaded neck-laces, their most important possession is cattle. A man's wealth and status in the community is determined by the number of cattle owned.

The morani are men between the ages of 18–26 who are not married. Their job is to protect the community from enemies as well as protect the cows from wild animals. The morani tradi-tionally travel with the cattle to find water and better grazing.

Conflicts between the Maasai morani and Christians had been brewing for some time, but came to the surface August 1 when the young warriors stormed Olopuko Baptist Church. More than 70 morani sounded the war cry as they descended on the church. One Pentecostal church was totally destroyed in a similar attack.

Tidenberg said the young warriors were fighting to keep cul-tural distinctives that are in direct conflict with God's Word.

"Most of the conflict deals with the very promiscuous prac-tices among the warrior (morani) class as well as polygamy," Tidenberg said. "The conflict has also come as many Chris-tians are no longer seeing the need for the "laibon"—witch doc-tor—and his powers. As Christians have matured, they have begun to stand firm in many of these areas."

While missionaries are not trying to change the culture, Tidenberg said he and fellow missionaries are teaching the truth through God's Word.

Since the government has indicated support for the non-Christian Maasai, there is concern that Christians will have

more difficulties in the days ahead. A special conference of
local pastors took place at the Tidenberg home as leaders tried
to find a peaceful resolution.

During the uprisings, a group of volunteers from Mobile,
Alabama, have trekked through many of the villages praying
and sharing. They have covered much of Maasailand on foot—
almost 100 miles—to pray for God to continue working among
this people group.

Tidenberg said the volunteers saw many saved despite the
vocal and physical resistance by the morani. One of the men
that prayed to receive Christ was a very influential witch doctor.

The largest battle came the first day of the uprising when
70 men stormed the Olopuko Baptist Church. The morani beat
the unarmed church members with clubs and spears. A cry
went up from the warriors proclaiming that "black blood or
white blood" would be shed.

Tidenberg and local Christians tried to fight back, but soon
realized that God's power was more powerful than physical
weapons. The group stepped back and prayed.

"The battle continued around us as a story from the Old
Testament began to unfold—confusion of the enemy," Tidenberg said. "The army Gideon fought against was confused and
fought themselves while Gideon's army stood and watched.
That is exactly what happened."

As the fighting Maasai continued to battle, the small Christian group moved forward and stood at peace in the midst of
the fight. For unknown reasons, the Maasai began to retreat.
The Christians were left standing, unharmed and thankful for
God's protection.

After the battle, Tidenberg was able to speak to the morani.
He met with the group for two hours, but they were determined
that the church was to be closed and houses burned down if the
believers met in homes. They wanted no Christian witness in
that area.

The missionary told the warriors that closing the church
building would not remove the church.

"The church will grow stronger," Tidenberg said. "I expressed to them that this is not a struggle with customs or culture. It is not that the world around them is changing, but it is a hardness of their hearts that has caused this conflict.

The door for the gospel has been wide open in Maasailand and Tidenberg asked prayer warriors throughout the world to pray for its continued openness. In an August 12 meeting between Christians, elders in the villages, and morani, the missionary's prayer was answered.

The elders in the meeting spoke in the meeting and gave testimony. Several morani stood up and admitted they were wrong, asked the Christians to stay, and asked for forgiveness. They requested the Christians to share what Christ has done and to help them fully understand.

"We had asked for prayers that the doors would not close because of this heated conflict between the Maasai culture and Christianity. We never expected such intervention," Tidenberg said. "The main result of this meeting? The doors for evangelism and church planting in this area have never been thrown as wide open as they are now."

Christianity and culture

Because in years past some people have equated Christianity with American religious culture—all churches should have steeples, all music should sound like Western hymns—missions today can sometimes carry a stigma of being a tool of changing culture rather than hearts. But the Southern Baptist missionaries to the Maasai in Kenya and Tanzania did not come to convert villages into little Americas—they came to share the gospel. Bob Calvert summed up the missionary desire: "Let the Maasai be the Maasai." What does this mean in practice? The Maasai Christians decide what parts of their culture do or do not harmonize with their Christian beliefs. Young Christian Maasai men who reject the

"One day we will see so many Maasai in heaven . . ." —Joy Cox, missionary to Maasai

warrior system offer one example of this change of culture, but it is a change that comes from the Maasai, not from the missionaries.

Other changes in Maasai life include the beginning of a decrease in female circumcision and more schooling for children. But Maasai Christians still value their cattle, still have a deep harmony with nature, and bring their love of music and stories to their Christian worship. A few universal church practices are emphasized, and these all exist in the Maasai church: proclamation of God's word, music, discipleship, giving of time and material goods, and fellowship.

The future among the Maasai

When William Carey, legendary missionary to India, first spoke of his evangelistic burden to English Christians, they attempted to quash his enthusiasm for spreading the gospel to all people. They told him God did not need his help if He wished anyone outside the already-Christian world to know of Him. Carey did not let that attitude stop him; and largely because of his determination, the gospel has spread across the globe.

Still, there are people who have not heard of Jesus and His love for them. There are people, like the Maasai, who have heard and who want the rest of their people to have the same opportunity. Patient years of work are paying off. "We are seeing many of the Maasai clans on the brink of what could be a great church planting movement," says Bob Calvert. At least one Maasai area, where David and Renee Crane are located, is already seeing vigorous growth.

What does the future hold for the Maasai, who number more than one-quarter of a million people? Only God knows exactly what the future holds; but from all indications, the gospel will continue to spread through Maasailand, even in the face of persecution, resistance to anything seen as an outside force, and criticism that Christianity is somehow a threat to Maasai culture. Missionaries and Maasai Christians need many things to meet this God-given opportunity and overcome these negative forces, but their prime need is the prayers of dedicated fellow Christians around the world. While missionaries desire prayer for their own needs, they also want prayer for Maasai Christians as they move into their rightful places of leadership in the Maasai churches, while the missionaries move further and further into the background.

Change is coming for all the Maasai; many of them see it happening already. Some are ready to embrace political and economic changes, such as the necessity to put down roots and give up their seminomadic wandering. Others want to fight the outside world, while others do not yet see the changes that are encroaching on the life their people have lived for centuries. The spread of the gospel is part of this overall change. But while some changes will affect only portions of the Maasai's world, the gospel can affect them for eternity. Missionary Joy Cox sums up the future for the Maasai well:

"We love watching God at work among Maasai because it was not very long ago that this people group fully resisted the gospel. These days, so many Maasai continue to listen to God's word and receive His salvation!

"One day we will see so many Maasai in heaven who we have known on earth. So it is a pleasure to minister among people whom God has chosen to bring revival and a harvest for His kingdom here on earth and in heaven."

5

THE MAASAI, JESUS, AND YOU

Your love has a broken wing if it cannot fly across the sea.—Maltbie Babcock

Well, this is a great work. Glad to hear about it."

These cannot be the last words Southern Baptists speak after learning about the Maasai. Neither can they be the last words you speak. Now you know the Maasai, not as a stereotype, but as a people, as individuals God loves. Now you know the missionaries who serve God among them. They are no longer just "the study missionaries." You can call them by name: David, Bob, Renee, Joy . . .

And if you are a Christian, you know Jesus. His Spirit lives in you and speaks to you about people like the Maasai. It is up to you to decide if you will listen to His Spirit in you.

Henry Blackaby, author of *Experiencing God,* wrote in *Called and Accountable*: "Once as a child of God you know an initiative of God in your life, you must immediately, and without resistance or discussion, respond obediently to all God is directing."

58

What is God directing you to do about the spiritual and physical needs of the Maasai?

Pray

IMB staff member Randy Sprinkle is a former missionary to the African country of Lesotho and the author of *Until the Stars Appear*, a story about the power of prayer on the missions field. He wrote, "Satan knows that work without prayer is work without power, and from that he has nothing to fear."

The missionaries and Maasai Christians, like missionaries and Christians all over the world, want and need the prayers of their Christian brothers and sisters. Prayer needs have been highlighted throughout this book, but following is a more concise list for your personal prayer use.

Pray for the missionaries
•Safety in traveling the dusty, often dangerous dirt roads
•Physical health and strength in an area where stomach ailments, eye infections, and back problems, among other things, can plague missionaries
•Patience when resources like water and electricity are not plentiful
•Peace of mind about relatives left behind in the US
•Peace of mind about children away at boarding school
•Comfort in times of isolation and loneliness
•Wisdom to know what to do for children and family members
•Growth in faith, biblical knowledge, and love

For the Maasai Christians
•Strength to put away ungodly practices
•Faithfulness in the face of criticism and hostility
•Greater understanding of the Bible
•Growth in faith and spiritual understanding as they plant and lead churches

- Wisdom to know how to best present the gospel to their people
- Health and strength to face drought, plague, and other adversities
- Harmony and growth in existing churches
- More Maasai to obey God's call to become church leaders

For other Maasai
- More churches to be started and sustained
- Maasai warriors to be open to hearing the gospel
- Health ministries to help Maasai women and children

For all Maasai
- Rain to end drought conditions and ease their suffering
- Protection for their cattle from theft, disease, and drought
- Ability to face their changing society

Become an advocate

An advocate is one who speaks out on behalf of the needs of others, especially those who have no voice. While the Maasai have a voice within their own society, they need for their brothers and sisters in Christ in the rest of the world to remember them and support them. You can promote concern for the Maasai in several ways:
- Share this book with other believers.
- Place this book in your church media library.
- Write a review of this book for your church newsletter or bulletin.
- Lead the International Mission Study in your church.
- Make the prayer requests from this book available to other individuals and groups, and encourage them to join you in praying for the Maasai.
- Create a bulletin board or interest center about the Maasai in your church.

- Lead your church to adopt the Maasai. This could include regular prayer for them, letters and gifts to the Maasai missionaries, and regular updates about the progress of church planting among the Maasai.
- Research the Internet, newspapers and magazines, and broadcast news sources for new information on the Maasai.
- Write letters or send prayergrams to the missionaries in this study. Their addresses are available from the missionary directory published by the IMB (check the IMB Web site: www.imb.org). (Remember, the missionaries will be receiving a lot of correspondence, which can take a great deal of time to answer. Write, but let them know you do not expect a response.)

Give

Ethlene Boone Cox, a former president of Woman's Missionary Union and one of its great leaders, said, "Giving is one way of living with all your might." By giving sacrificially and cheerfully to missions, you help the missionaries who are helping the Maasai and other people groups around the world experiencing a surge in church growth, as well as those in other fields. By giving, you are supporting the growth of God's kingdom and helping lay the foundation for future growth in places that so far have only been claimed in prayer and faith. Your giving is an investment in eternity.

Many other resources contain general ideas about how to gauge your missions giving. The following ideas can tie your giving to what you have learned about the Maasai. As you give, you can visualize the people you will be helping.

Conserve water

Because of their own lack of water, and even more because of the drought that has devastated the Maasai, the missionaries are very aware of the need to be good stewards of their water supplies. While you can't mail your rainwater to the Maasai, you can pray for them when you turn on a water tap. You can thank God for the water you have, and be a good steward of it. You can make a conscious effort to lower your water bill, and dedicate the money saved to missions.

Eat meatless meals
Although the Maasai love to eat meat, they are not wasteful of their animal wealth. They know how to conserve meat. When you cut back on meat consumption and eat more vegetarian meals, you save money for missions and get the added bonus of better health!

Weigh priorities
As you have learned, the Maasai are not caught up in the need to have large buildings, or even any buildings, before they call themselves a church. A shed with a roof and some branches for pews, or even the shade of a large tree, is all the physical structure most Maasai churches have. Western Christians could learn from them.

No one is suggesting a church building is bad. Churches use their facilities for education, recreation, and ministry as well as worship. But the needs of missions work among people like the Maasai must be weighed against the pressures of keeping up and redecorating a church building. When an expenditure is suggested for the church building, ask, "Is this necessary? Could the carpet last another year? Could we do some of the painting (or plumbing, or masonry) ourselves?" Money saved on church buildings can further the building of God's kingdom in other places. It is good stewardship to care for the building God has entrusted to your church. But as someone once said, "We must not wait until every church is lighted with an elegant chandelier before we send the lamp of God's word to the nations that sit in darkness."

Volunteer

The Maasai team welcomes volunteers, especially groups, which they use extensively in their work. Volunteers can do construction projects or hold medical, dental, or animal husbandry clinics, so there is a place for doctors, nurses, agricultural specialists, carpenters, masons, preachers, and teachers. Laity, from youth through senior adults, can help with evangelism, discipleship training, prayer-walking, and construction. Individuals can fill many roles, depending upon the missionary's need. Contact the International Mission Board[1] about needs that volunteer teams can fill, or about individual service.

[1]Contact the International Mission Board's Volunteer Office at P. O. Box 6767, Richmond, VA 23230.

APPENDIX

CHURCH PLANTING MOVEMENT

"First, CPMs are from God, not man. CPMs are God-inspired, influenced, and driven by the Holy Spirit and not man. But God uses His people to work in CPMs as His witnesses, His hands, His feet, and His mouth. But CPMs originate from God, by God, for God."—David Cox, missionary to the Maasai

---

The International Mission Board's definition of a church planting movement (CPM) is: "a rapid and exponential increase of indigenous churches planting churches within a given people group or population segment."[1]

What does that mean in plain English? David Garrison of the International Mission Board (IMB) has provided the following insights. By breaking the definition into small, bite-sized parts, we can understand what a CPM is and why it is important in the future of work among the Maasai and other people groups.

A CPM is marked by rapid, exponential growth. Over the centuries, an area can develop many churches, even be saturated with churches; but when God is energizing a CPM, the growth is quick. *Exponential* is simply a math term meaning that churches grow by multiplying rather than by adding one or two at a time (the incremental approach). One church becomes two, two become four, four become eight, etc. Professional church planters can add churches one at a time, but exponential growth only comes when churches are dedicated to starting other new churches. (Does this mean having full-time church planters is bad? Certainly not, as you will see below.)

A CPM creates *indigenous* churches, meaning they are created within the people group rather than from outside. They are churches that belong culturally to that people group and spring up from within that group. Of course, the gospel always starts from outside a group or an individual. Areas that today are considered to be heavily Christian are so because someone took the gospel to them. Saint Patrick was a missionary to the Irish. Paul was a missionary to Asia Minor. And as Maltbie Babcock pointed out, "We are the children of the converts of foreign missionaries; and fairness means that I must do to others as men once did to me."[2]

> "A CPM is *not* churches growing by splintering off due to disagreements. A CPM is a movement energized by God wherein existing churches start new churches."— David Cox, missionary to the Maasai

With a CPM, that message brought into a group is then spread by the group and results in churches started by the group rather than by outside forces.

"A Church Planting Movement is also more than a revival of pre-existing churches. Revivals are highly desirable, but they're not Church Planting Movements. Evangelistic crusades and witnessing programs may lead thousands to Christ, and that's wonderful, but it isn't the same as a Church Planting

Movement. Church Planting Movements feature churches rapidly reproducing themselves," writes David Garrison.[3]

Also, as missionary David Cox points out, a CPM is *not* churches growing by splintering off due to disagreements. A CPM is a movement energized by God wherein existing churches start new churches.

"However," says David Garrison, "a Church Planting Movement is not simply an increase in the number of churches, even though this also is positive. A Church Planting Movement occurs when the vision of churches planting churches spreads from the missionary and professional church planter into the churches themselves, so that by their very nature they are winning the lost and reproducing themselves."[4]

The shape and history of individual church planting movements varies, but there are ten universal elements.[5]

1. Prayer
Prayer by and for the missionary is vital to reaching a people group. By having a vital prayer life, the missionary models the importance of prayer to the new church and its leaders.

2. Abundant gospel sowing
"Every church planting movement is accompanied by abundant sowing of the gospel," writes David Garrison. While mass media evangelism can play an effective part in this sowing, personal evangelism that testifies to the life-changing power of the gospel is crucial. In areas where governments or cultural pressures have suppressed Christian witness, CPMs have not arisen. As 2 Corinthians 9:6 (NIV) says, "Remember this: Whoever sows sparingly will also reap sparingly, and whoever sows generously will also reap generously." Sharing the gospel is crucial to a CPM.

3. Intentional church planting

At the beginning of every CPM stands someone who had a strategy of deliberate church planting. These strategies are not always foolproof. They are the best someone could do with the knowledge and resources they had at the time. If Christians wait for the perfect set of circumstances, the perfect strategy, the perfect amount of resources before acting, they will be waiting forever.

On the other hand, missionary strategists spend much time studying the people group and prayerfully looking for the best ways to introduce the gospel to that people group.

4. Scriptural authority

Scriptural authority answers every need for guidance arising in new churches. Most people groups who have experienced a CPM have had the Bible translated into their heart language in either oral or written form.

5. Local leadership

A missionary or team of missionaries trains local leadership. That local leadership will eventually train other leadership. As a CPM progresses, the missionary's role changes as local Christians take the lead.

6. Lay leadership

"Church planting movements are driven by lay leaders." These lay leaders fit the profile of their people group. In other words, they are typical of their group and fit into the same economic and educational status as most of the people in their group. Most are bivocational, having a job that supports themselves and their families, while at the same time serving the church.

7. Cell or house churches

A cell church shares a structured network with other churches under the authority of a unifying church. A house church usually has no link with other house churches to a unifying church. While the cell church format helps ensure doctrinal conformity, house churches face less threat of suppression by governments. Neither type of church is dependent on a church building.

8. Churches planting churches
In the beginning of a CPM, churches are begun by missionaries or missionary-trained church planters who are national Christians. As a CPM develops, however, the churches take the initiative to reproduce, making a CPM a grassroots effort.

9. Rapid reproduction
Every CPM evidenced so far is characterized by the rapid starting of new churches.

10. Healthy churches
According to church growth experts, there are five core functions in a healthy church. CPM churches share these functions: worship, evangelistic and missionary outreach, education and discipleship, ministry, and fellowship. It is hard for a church not to grow when these functions are at the heart of its existence. Among certain people groups, missionary outreach by their indigenous churches means the gospel will be taken to places and people unreached by Western efforts.

A question of heresy

If members of a people group instead of international missionaries or North American missionaries paid by that country's missions entity begin new churches, will the churches be thoroughly Christian? Is there not a risk of heresy?

The five church purposes listed above—worship, evangelistic and missionary outreach, education and discipleship, ministry, and fellowship—will help keep a church stable. If a church fulfills these five purposes and stays rooted and grounded in the Word of God, there is no more reason to fear heresy in a CPM than in any other type of church planting.

Ten Common Factors

There are ten common, but not universal, factors found in CPMs, according to David Garrison.[6] Many of these can be found in the Maasai experience.

1. Worship in the heart language.
"Nothing reveals a people group's worldview as much as an intimate knowledge of their heart language," writes David Garrison. The heart language is the language learned and spoken by the people group and seen as their own, even if they may be fluent in another "trade language" with which they communicate with outsiders. For the Maasai, their heart language is Maa, but services are also conducted in Kiswahili.

2. Evangelism has communal implications.
It can be hard for Westerners steeped in the worldview of rugged individualism to understand how much community affects a CPM. Families or whole villages may make decisions of faith at the same time because to do something outside family or community is unthinkable. With the Maasai, while individual women have made professions of faith, it is often preferable for the men to discuss the decision with the family (sometimes for long periods of time) so the whole family may respond to the gospel at the same time.

3. Rapid incorporation of new converts into the church.
New believers are encouraged to immediately begin helping with church planting and evangelism. Discipleship is ongoing.

4. Passion and fearlessness.
A CPM is marked by a passion for sharing the gospel and
boldness in the face of hostility and persecution. The story
by IMB missionary Sue Sprenkle (p. 50) is one example of
the courage and dedication of Maasai believers.

5. A price to pay for believers.
North American Christians have little concept of the price
Christian believers pay in many parts of the world.
Church planting movements often erupt in areas hostile
to the gospel. These Christians are inspired and comforted
by the example of New Testament believers, who also suf-
fered persecution for their faith.

6. Perceived leadership crisis or spiritual vacuum in society.
This crisis or vacuum may be created through war, natural
disaster, or cultural chaos. In these instances people grope
for meaning and structure, knowing that materialism has
not saved them. The Maasai now face huge cultural
changes due to demands on the land and greater inter-
action with other peoples.

7. On-the-job training for church leadership.
The upsurge in new churches does not allow for the luxury of leadership spending years in academic training.
While leaders lead, they receive training such as Theological Education by Extension (TEE).

8. Leadership authority is decentralized.
Church planting movements are too vigorous to allow for
numerous levels of authority. Cell churches must be free
to make their own decisions to maintain growth and
vitality.

9. Outsiders keep a low profile.
As soon as possible missionaries foster believers as church

leaders and become mentors and helpers. The goal is for the people group eventually to have complete leadership without the aid of missionaries.

10. Missionaries suffer.
Missionary service is not luxurious on any field, but missionaries associated with CPMs seem to have a high level of suffering. David Garrison writes, "Whatever the cause, the disproportionate degree of suffering by missionaries engaged in church planting movements is noteworthy. Missionaries intent on this course of action are well-advised to be on their guard, to watch, fight, and pray."

[1]David Garrison, "Church Planting Movements" (Richmond, VA: International Mission Board, 1999), 1.
[2]Frank Mead, *The Encyclopedia of Religious Quotations* (Westwood, NJ: Fleming H. Revell), 308.
[3]Garrison, "Church Planting Movements," 8.
[4]Ibid., 9–10.
[5]Ibid., 33–36.
[6]Ibid., 37–40.

About the author
Cathy Butler is a freelance writer and a former editor for Woman's Missionary Union, SBC. She writes for missions education periodicals, including *Missions Mosaic* and *Dimension* magazines, and is the author of *Wonderful Words of Life; I Can Do That!;* and *Servants of the Banquet.* She has served as WMU director of Shelby Baptist Association in Alabama and as Alabama WMU state recording secretary. She currently lives in west Alabama with her husband and two sons.